Toy Firing Squad

poems by tom chandler

WIND PUBLICATIONS

International Standard Book Number 978-1-893239-70-8
Library of Congress Control Number 2007942892

First edition

Acknowledgements

Thanks to the following journals, in which these poems first appeared.

American Literary Review – "Psalm," "The Family Name"
Antietam Review – "The Partial Truth"
Asheville Poetry Review – "Darwin Awards"
Atlanta Review – "This Story"
Boulevard – "First Poem," "High Dark Windows"
Brown Literary Review – "Be Thanking"
Cimarron Review – "Kaddish for Bob"
Crab Creek Review – "Progress Reports"
Cream City Review – "Alarmed"
Cumberland Poetry Review – "Curriculum Vitae," "Burning Leaves"
Dalhousie Review – "Another Satisfied Victim"
The Evansville Review – "Tao of the Yo"
Georgia State University Review – "North Providence"
Green Mountains Review – "Dear Wind,"

Helix – "Sidekicks," "The Greatest Day in the World", "The Persistence of Memory," "Everybody," "Aftermath"
International Poetry Review – "Phyllis"
The Literary Review – "Sample Citizen"
The Macguffin – "The Sleeping Porch"
MiPoesis.com – "Night Books," "Heartleaf Popple"
Paterson Literary Review – "Backyard Bomb Shelter"
The Pinch – "Seaside Motel"
Poet Lore – "Uncle Philippe"
Poetry International – "Midweek Poem," "My Martini"
PoetrySky.com – "Hard Music"
Potomac Review – "Mrs. Impossible"
Roger – "Our Fathers"
Runes – "Skipping Stones"
South Dakota Review – "Camp Morton Prison, 1862," "The Birder"
Spoon River Poetry Review – "The Luthier"
Sulphur River Literary Review – "Roadkill"
Wisconsin Review – "Blue State of Mind"
Yalobusha Review – "Crank Calls," "Pregnant Girls in High School"

"Toy Firing Squad" was included in *The Gift of Experience*, an anthology published by the *Atlanta Review*.

"So Much Depends Upon" was included in the "Best of the Decade" issue of *Hawaii Pacific Review*.

"For David Cicilline" was commissioned as the official poem of the Providence, Rhode Island mayoral inauguration. It was also included in *The Other Side of Sorrow*, an anthology published by the New Hampshire Poetry Society.

"For Charles Sullivan" was commissioned by the Rhode Island Council for the Humanities.

"Poem to Honor the Zinman Urinals" was commissioned by the benefactor of a men's restroom in the Van Pelt-Dietrich Library Center at the University of Pennsylvania.

Photo collages: "The Parisians," "Des Amis" by Tom Chandler

for Lisa

Contents

III

IV

I

Curriculum Vitae

Whatever is is is of little concern;
       I lie between fronds of grass-colored grass

that ripple in wind like pictures you see of rippling
       grass and am happy, uselessly, helplessly so;

       O the tens of thousands of meals I have eaten;
       O beloved nutrients I have rented

to squeeze through guts of varying dimension
       for miles and furtively enter my blood.

       O the tens of thousands of kisses, shelved
       in the attic of ten thousand books.

O rippling life, how like the grass
       you might see in a picture of grass

       smoothed by meaningless wind
       and the absence of someone like me.

First Poem

My father sat in the stern, sternly
guiding us into the current,
eyes shaded by a battered hat
as I sat in the bow, dizzy with joy
at riding the river, at being this boy
and at noon we beached on a sandbar
and sandwich in hand watched
the ducks fly away quacking fear;
my father offered me sips of his beer
and then went for a swim
and stripped bare I glanced
at the places his body grew hair
and he said that I would as well
all too soon and that night we sat
silent and stared at the moon rising
up through the forest and I felt
the dark breeze lift the light from
the day like campfire smoke
out over the river and forever,
forever away.

Progress Reports

I

He shed two tears,
poured them in a peanut shell,
carefully taped it shut,
mailed it in a box.

By the time it reached her
the tears had evaporated;
she cried as she spread
peanut butter on her toast,
sipped her morning coffee,
checked her mail.

II

He gently swatted
the mosquito that bit her knee,
so softly she hadn't noticed.

Later, he searched the ground
where she had sat, found the
tiny crumpled body, froze it
in an ice cube which he saved
for cocktail hour.

The Partial Truth

When the cages finally shed their bars
and let us climb inside the wind
to heal the wounds of distance,
the sky will finally smile down
the way it would if it could.

And when dogs dance and trees break
into song to lift the wings of the tired bird
who hasn't flown in years,
the bullets will drip at last like tears
from the barrel of the gun.

The ears are cauldrons
into which the world pours dark music
and the heart just a filling
for the chest's cavity
and there is absolutely nothing

but the tiny mouths of words
to kiss each eyelash of each eye
and soothe you as you read.

Another Satisfied Victim

We can't see electrons buzzing
around their orbits in a piece of wood,
can't grasp all that movement
bustling toward decay.

They say the light from all the stars
would flood the night if we could see it,
but the universe is still too young, the most
distant sparks haven't yet had time to touch us.

We cannot see the heart of the shark,
who must keep moving to breathe,
or understand the tyrant, who pets his dog
and stares into the mirror,

or reason with the hurricane,
which does not comprehend its lungs,
or the years when rain decides to hide
its face from the forest's flames,

the thousand ways to praise the unseen,
the thousand ways to fall to our knees
and kiss the visible ground.

Sample Citizen

Because he owned a television
almost the size of the moon
he told himself the moon was
actually the size that it appeared to be,
a tarnished dime on tattered cloth;
because he lived in Saginaw or Omaha
he took it out on the family dog
when no one was around and sat
before bed in his roofless yard,
its small ground surveyed each night
in his dream as he powerslept
his powersleep so desperately
his brain would clench and squeak
until the house and roofless yard
were two feet deep in raining dimes
and he could finally watch TV
by simply staring where the moon
had been or had been thought to be.

A Visit With Uncle Philippe

We sit at court on folding chairs,
watch him scratch his balls
through his bathrobe, long past
all small discretions
or the itch of little words.
He's haloed in thin light this night,
not sick just ninety-six; thinks
he's earned the right to whine at will
in phlegmy French, says English gives him
heartburn, and his adam's apple's plainly lost
for good inside that frayed sleeve of a voice.
There were twelve in my family, he tells the gray
grandaughter hovering with applesauce and spoon,
now there is merely me, merely me, merely me.
He sighs a deeply Gallic sigh
and looks around disgustedly.
Why can't I die?
My life has been an opera, a great novel.
He twists his scrawny vulture neck,
squints and sniffs the hospital smell, asks
will hell be as magnificent as this?

Kaddish for Bob

It was snowing hard when the rabbi said
to shovel the dirt back into the grave

and requested the first shovelful be made
with the back of the graveside spade

and a man stepped away from
the rest of us, bare head

snow frosted, and grabbed the handle
and tucked to the work, shouldering dirt

as fast as he could, which thumped
on the coffin in a broken beat behind

the wind sweeping down from the sky
through the stark reach of branches

while he stabbed helplessly over
and over into the whitening earth.

Night Books

Words rise up from the pages, fold into the silence
and beyond, lift past the cone of shaded light

that guides you sightful with its single
white hand, its fingers stretched from rooms of sleep,

walls of mountains shedding granite into oceans,
into oceans waving at the stars, an aurora borealis

forming music out of sky, the stories of night books,
the melancholy sex, the laughter after dreaming,

the dreaming faded to a stain of meaning splashed
across blank paper.

Kayak Journal

A thousand yards out I paused, saw all that loose blue sky
and how the sea I sat on was a version of air and how
the wind stroked my hair like a woman's hand
as ducks and brants flashed by and a jellyfish
pulsed its song of joy about how I could never die
when floating in this painting of so much beauty
and so what if I did.

Whale Breath

The fog thinned as we were sailing over Stellwagen Bank,
which looked exactly the same as when we weren't
till a minke broke the surface only six feet from the bow,
spouted as the wind stiffed and splashed that mist flat full
in my face, wetting my cheeks, making my eyes sting,
ancient stew of everything, spewed from the lungs
of a wild whale and sucked inside my own.

That night in bed I could still taste its breath,
sharp with rot, feel the swell beneath the mattress,
the slowly waving arms of kelp, then
something that has no name as I slid under
and under the sad wordless songs.

Skipping Stones

He could displace the face of any lake,
barely break the surface, convince the water
to kiss the rock, convince the rock to resist.

He'd search cracked shale beds baking in the sun,
culling hydrodynamic from asymmetric,
the millions of stones from the millions of years

lying smoothed and wind-brushed in the hush of noon.
And yes there was passion in the way he caressed
his perfect decision, sucked a finger to test the breeze,

then skimmed light with just the right english
to skip it eight, ten, a dozen times before it sank
as I watched the concentric circles of ripples

intersect from each step the stone had taken
to form the secret map of the world
that nobody knows how to read.

Backyard Bomb Shelter

A flat black bulkhead flat in the grass
back behind the garbage cans out over
near the swing set, just past the sandbox
where the cat did her business and Mike
blew up ants with cherry bombs
his dad had smuggled home.

Inside were rows of cans and plastic jugs
of water, a pile of rolled up sleeping bags
and a dark green Coleman stove and it was
1961 and Mike's dad kept his gun collection
oiled and clean in the corner, glad the family
had this place to wait for the world to end.

On humid August afternoons I'd sit inside
its welcome shadows pretending it was
raining missiles everywhere and everyone
was suddenly zapped to white powder
that glowed for a flash before vanishing
into nothing at all while I watched
Mike make spiders shrivel gently
at the soft tiny tongue of candle flame.

Dear Wind,

We sense what you suggest
as you drift fingers through a stranger's hair,
give conversation to unfallen oak leaves,
form to fallen snow.

All night you squeak through
leaks in the clapboards, trying to tell us
how you died in the heart of the ocean,
rose up in resurrection to the wild sky,

carried birds to where they did or didn't want to go,
left the smell of Africa across Vermont
and brought the song of the Asian steppes
to leafy towns in Connecticut.

Blue curtain of nothing, you are the only church,
impossible to touch, we hear your words
reflected off the flags you kiss, the gravestones
you topple in your passing.

Our Fathers

Bo sucked the cherry brandy bottle
thirty five years ago in another state
and handed it over, back when we were
so young we believed that dawn
changes everything and stayed up all night
to prove it, killing off the present, waiting
for a future we had already decided
would look like the sky only more so
as we passed the brandy, sitting in a car
in a parking lot deep in the past that was
too sweet and boozy the way boys
who are twenty and not yet men but who
should be shouldn't be but were, though
of course, the pages of this tired story
are worn now from all the trying to thumb
ahead, to skip past the part where the boys
became sober, became old, came to know
the meaningless welcome of empty hands
in empty pockets while all the while
our fathers watched impossibly
from their pillows of stone.

II

North Providence

The kid who quit school understands the ass side
of the city, knows what lies in the weeds behind
the gas station, knows all about the broken condoms
and cigarette butts, the bits of plastic packing,
the bright green snake seen for only half a second.

Deer tracks pock the freeway islands where
the homeless men toast his health with aftershave;
along the tracks coyotes smirk against
the backdrop of a thousand smoggy roofs
and pockets of marsh erupt past the chain link
and the broken eyes of factories
closed before he was born.

Once, he saw a huge brown owl swoop low
through the sprouted bramble of sumac
and cracked asphalt,
looking like a dream about flight.
Even now, kicking the curb as he scuffles
toward the rest of his life, he remembers.

This Story

I think I'd like to die in Rhode Island someday,
wading in the bay in rotten sneakers at slack water,
my basket partly full of clams, my eyes focused
on their little air holes in the sand

on a late afternoon on a late August weekday,
with clouds herding up along the south horizon,
banking off toward Block Island and beyond,
and I will swat at a greenhead buzzing near my neck

and fall into the slant of four o'clock sun beneath
the half-inch ripples of the incoming tide and close out
this story, except for the postscript where I'm later found
by two guys floating by in a rented canoe eating meatball subs

who took the day off to drink some beer on the bay
and never thought they'd read about themselves in the paper
or that night tell their wives about the body they found
face down in the muck and how the police questioned them

about the beer and so this story will pass from mouth
to ear across the towns I lived in, the places where I rode my bike
to the store to buy my mother's cigarettes and Mike Boyle's brother
will recall the time I broke into the school that night with Mike

and Sheryl Pannebaker's father will fold the newspaper in his lap
and think it was a good thing she married a chiropractor and across
the football field near the high school a couple of kids will stop
laughing and look up at the sky for no reason while out on the bay

a sudden piece of wind will blow in from the sea and the spot
near the shore where I felt this story collapse in my chest
will be commemorated by mud and the stink of low tide
and the gray sails of circling gulls.

The Three Sisters

— ancient Wampanoag staple food

Corn, beans and squash are set out before me,
along with the dangled carrot of contentment,
and the sun, harvest smudge, glints through
clean windows to wash this room
in November browns.

And we thank Thee that the cornstalks stretched
to sturdy poles for the beans to climb, that the corn
leaves fanned out to shade the squash
and the beans added nitrogen for them all,
that ten centuries before this little minute

proud, grateful men ate exactly this,
understood the wind, spoke the poems
of deep forest in nightfall, watched
the three sisters hold hands in the clay pot
and dance to an ancestor's spirit in the flames.

The Darwin Awards

Every day somebody drowns
in a damp hankie,
sneaks inside a safe to hide,
sticks a fork in the toaster,
touches up mascara
in the rearview mirror
and still the reckless world rolls on,
set to see us fall, weaving gunshots
through the future, stringing cancer
from the tree limbs, building ever-sleeker
cars with weaker brakes while hearts
continue their iambic rumble,
sparks crackle down a brain stem,
both lung's trees in constant bloom,
each breath a defiance and
despite the color-coded warning,
the childproof cap, the lead-off story,
the surgeon general's report
and the tire's squeal we persist
in being born completely naked,
without crash helmet, kneepads
or a prayer.

Pregnant Girls in High School

Would lean against their lockers
with their bellies pressed into
the anguish of algebra while

I would try to look indifferent
passing by their lives on my way
to fail another true false test.

Their boyfriends were too tough
for football or laughter and lounged
in the hallways like sullen sultans,

hands carved into permanent fists,
their careless faces unfolding as men
who would soon leave forever to work

fitting pipe on their backs in the dirt
or riding jackhammers inside clouds
of noise while the fast-faded mothers

of the babies they'd fathered
smoked down to the filter and
ironed the sheets in the shadows.

Song & Dance Man

Now he's hunched with the rest
over lunch of nuked soup in this
clattery cafeteria, cheek bones
honed to a whore's whisper,
the sad map face folded in thirds
and each third saggy as shit but
back when he was hitting on those
summer circuit waitresses he had
real teeth and a tune to polish
every minute of the night so
of course she made him sing it
right at her and yes he made her
howl when he left, all slouchy
cigarette with no paunch then
and plenty punch, brassy jazz
on three martinis when he'd drop
to one knee, spread arms wide enough
to take in everything and all its loser
history and belt one out to make you
see how raggedy and right he loved
his smiley bad self.

For David Cicilline

Who would've thought that hope still has wings?
We've been told by the television that hope is a broken tower,
a broken airplane, the echoes of thousands of lost broken voices.
We've been told that hope is a tunnel now,
a hole of scumbled mud,
something we must crawl through on our knees.

We've been told by bloody headlines
that we're supposed to spend our lives as anxious shadows
and lock our doors and unlock our luggage and lock our hearts
and unlock our guns and lock our words, and lock our words.

And who would've thought on such a pale, shaken planet
that hope is still a bird with long strong wings
that rests its flight on the tips of buildings
and calls its name out over everything that's genuine and fair
and honest and fresh and rising up into a morning sky.

It took us all our lives to stand here at last
on the brink of the present, this tiny chip
of time we are sharing right now.

After all we've been through and before all that's just about
        to happen,
who would've thought that hope still has wings?

For Charles Sullivan

Far above our amazed gazes
he raises his bright life,

a weightlessness he offers up
offhandedly; above his head

a dozen juggled butcher knives
and flaming torches hover;

he smiles behind his famous glasses
while 93 million miles away

the sun has paused
to blast its gases higher

so that all of us might clearly see
how casual is his genius

posing easily past gravity,
the scars he teases back to sleep,

the face of grace washed clean with light,
the astonishing beauty of human beings.

Phyllis

Ugly name hissed
through front teeth
that tastes as sharp
as cola fizz;
I follow on my bike,
practice being invisible,
admiring her life
in the dappling light
the trees make;
taller than me,
a complicated grin
like the grid
of a suspension bridge,
breasts like adams apples;
I steal two Salems
from the purse left
on the kitchen counter,
share one in the cemetery
silence after school;
in bed that night I can feel
the shape the days make,
last week's homework
yet untouched, the chalk-
smeared backs of teachers
and Phyllis' frizzy nest of hair,
the rest of everything
melting into stars.

Gordon

We'd ring his doorbell six times a night
then run laughing as he cursed us
from the threshold of his loneliness,
which lived his life beside him
disguised as black silence in the hall.

We rattled his window with pebbles,
popped his Christmas lights in the street
as he howled his anguish at being
who he was
while his loneliness listened carefully
and we hooted back from the curb.

Later, he would lie in his bed
as his loneliness, which had begun
as solitude, spoke in a loud voice
and he would be torn awake
and sit bolt upright, shocked
at night's blanket

as we explored the cruelty
of being fourteen, slashed
the tires of tired sedans
while his loneliness watched us
from the trees.

Mrs. Impossible

She said she was washing her wings
in the dirt, tired of sifting the light
for the rest of us, tired of lifting
her beautiful self above each
melted Icarus, over rooftop ledges,
spires stiff with inspiration
poking the guts of the red city sky
and that is why she peeled the feathers
back from her shoulders, squatted
on the sidewalk with the dog turds
and broken glass, gazed with longing
at the crowds drifting past,
raised whispers of pain into broken
music and slowly wiped her fingertips
across her filthy skirt; she was
washing her wings in the dirt.

The Luthier

He shaved the spruce tops nearly translucent,
held each to his ear and plunked with his thumb
since dead spots are subtle and the wood
has to sing itself into becoming.

He showed us the necks he had hung in a row,
fretted with bars and smooth pearl inlays
to kiss the fingers of a future that waited inside
the hovering silence, ready to swirl through coils

of brain for miles, slip down past where someone
ends and this wood begins to become the pulse
of any stranger listening nearby and nothing
is stranger than that.

The Birder

Knows a long-toed stint when he sees one,
the yellowed legs and how the upper breast
is tinged rufous in bright summer, even knows
that rufous is a reddish sort of gray.

Knows its black streaks make it the darkest
of Alaskan peeps, those rare stragglers
who fly in from Eurasia every May and stay
along the western coast till summer goes,

pecking at pebbles, stubbing their long toes.
All night he dreams of life lists and faintly
purring chirps and whistles, identifies
the cross-hatched tracks of wrentits

and dippers, can tell the call of a creeper from
a thrasher in his sleep, knows with eyes closed
that a red knot is a sandpiper and a sandpiper just
another kind of peep, cares that Wilson's pharalope

is semi-palmated, hears the small flocks
on the guano-spattered rocks inside his head
as they sing, as they lift him through the ceiling
on those desperate hopeful pumping wings.

Camp Morton Prison, 1862

They crouched hard under the same sun glare
that spills itself down on our heads today,
though of course much hotter and more yellow.

These were torn men badly disguised as teenage boys
who had not had a bath in months, maybe years;
their tents were worn through with tears

and the sun blazed right into their eyes and five
chaws of tobacco would buy a mouse and a mouse
would buy five chaws and a loaf of bread was worth

two mice and two mice would get you a loaf of bread
and there had been no bread for a very long time
and as far as you could see was the stink of shit and death

and also a faint whiff that drifted like hope
from the earth to the sky whenever one of them
stirred the mouse stew.

… for my grandfather's grandfather

May 29th

Clear weather blows in
through the hole in the night,
we awaken to cardinals,
walls buttered by light and
when I stoop on the stoop
to retrieve the newspaper
its grief is still folded across
itself and I can smell good
coffee brewing up in all
directions, hear the rustle
of buttons being buttoned,
hair being brushed in hopeful
strokes in a hundred bedroom
mirrors as I stand unshaven
in my t-shirt and sweat pants
tasting the fresh sad perfect
morning blue sky which even
this early has autumn
inside of it, burning.

III

Seaside Motel

Hasn't been painted since Nixon was new
when a young couple on their way up the coast

and into the future rented this room and made
this baby who is now this man with thinning hair

who sits at this desk at the core of the city
and pecks this computer like a big beakless bird

hunting seeds yet pauses at the faint taste of salt
the faint snap of synapse in these coils of brain

as the wind off the winter surf snaps
these broken shutters this plywood nailed

to this window where his mother gazed out to sea
the next morning and knew everything.

Poem to Honor the Zinman Urinals

Once while hitching a rainy road
I stepped into the bushes for relief.
Looking down, I realized I was
watering a toad, who didn't seem
displeased, knowing I suppose that
if I had picked him up he would've
done the same to me, much as the sky
spilled itself on us both as we crouched
in the silence of dripping leaves
and the clouds soaked the man
who soaked the toad who
would've soaked the man.

Lost in contemplation I stand
before this urinal, cupped gently
in its porcelain embrace, taking
matters in hand for the fifth time
today in this dream I am having
of rain washing through me,
this dream I am having of being alive.

Yet Another New World

I toss the tattered cape across my shoulders,
conquistador of each beach I desire,
squint into sun the color of Mexico.

Soon, I know, the parrots will again squawk
my name through green corridors;
soon enough the local king will bring me
gold amulets spread on palm fronds,
my staked flag snapping in the onshore breeze.

And certainly, I've learned by now
how all these glory stories are the same,
the coming trek barefoot across the cactus plain,
all the dying for nothing but melons and corn,
the children sold before they are born.
But no one tells me what to do, and I must obey.

Blue State of Mind

I'm lost in a California of asphalt,
spilling brains and gasoline
across the wastes of Tennessee,
losing my virginity to depths of incredulity,
the icy peaks of war-torn Rhode Island.

O Lord of dying planets,
must we awaken in Texas
beneath a single star, curse the craven
Arkansas, crawl beneath the weight
of so much Alaska?

Each night I sleep with one eye open,
mortified at all the weird abundance,
the fat cheeks of Michigan,
the swelled hips of Montana,
flaccid Florida dribbling keys-

O dutiful capricious lies
for scrambled graves of pain,
for superpowers supersized above the brutal stain
of soft Athens and hard Sparta facing off
in acid rain.

So much depends upon

the blonde woman who drops a potato
in the supermarket parking lot where it rolls
beneath the 89 Dodge Ram with rust patches
near the left rear fender from contact with
too much road salt during the winter of 91
which was actually one of the mildest on record
though the driver tends to remember it
as the season he was fired from his job
at the aluminum window factory where
he had worked for nearly sixteen years
without promotion as he shifts into reverse
and backs over the potato which squishes
as softly as a dream's last breath and leaves
slick asphalt for the lot boy to slip on
as he pushes a train of shopping carts
and sprains his lumbar vertebrae just
days before he is scheduled to leave
for basic training to become the cool
killing machine he's always craved
but will now have to settle for someday
making assistant produce manager
and marrying a girl he almost loves just
as the blonde woman finds herself
one potato short with dinner guests
ringing the doorbell.

Everywhere I Travel

The sun is more important
and the sea wrack stink
sharper and the shops
dark and kindly, the woman
says may I help you sir in English
and when I ask how she knew
to do that before I'd even uttered
one word she tells me it is found
in the shoes, always in the shoes
for footwear is a patriotic act
and there is happiness hanging
upside down by its legs in all
the windows and the cool
breath of death to be winked at
and of course the food which is
fabulous everywhere on Earth.

Six Billion People

And all of you so beautiful
I want to bring you home with me
to sit close on the couch.

My invitation inserted in six billion bottles,
corked with bark from the final forest
and dropped in the ocean of my longing.

We would speak the language of no words,
pass the jug of our drunken joy
at being babies growing into death.

Sometimes, I know, life is stupid, pointless,
beside the point, but here's the point -
maybe we would fall

in love, settle down together,
share the wine, the bills,
the last of the oxygen and the remote.

Are We Alarmed Yet?

The alarm whoops began just after afternoon
began and began within minutes to fade into
the white noise that hums behind our lives and all
the neighbors heard it too as theme song to watching
the soaps while talking on the phone while screaming
at the kids to stop screaming while kicking the dog
while thinking of sex while eating.

By sunset the whooping had found the right rhythm
against which the day had all day been propped
and I thought I heard alarms call inside each thought
and the pulse matched my own and still the house
or car or whatever it was that admonished the world
and was denied cried its anguish to the bald sky
reflected in each window like a face with its eyes
shut tight and that night I was alarmed through
my dreams which were hot red as I slept
with all my might and fell desperately into the silence.

Psalm

Blessed is the glittery snow that falls some days
while the sun is shining, and blessed is the actor
who plays the honorable crook who is killed
by the actor who plays the flawed hero.

Blessed are the fish that wash up rotting
in unnoticed death on industrial shore,
and blessed is the hair on the barbershop floor,
happily intimate with strangers.

Your paper waits tomorrow on the pre-dawn porch,
blessed for how it has not been unfolded,
how its horrors are asleep, and blessed is the mosquito
that reddens with your precious blood
for the five hundred thousand year old song
it will carry to the sky.

Hard Music

The hammers of the builders
of the house across the street

sometimes fall by accident inside
the same beat, as if the rhythm

of our separate work can
melt without our knowing

into something far sleeker
than our laboring lives

and I wonder if the carpenters
are happy in themselves when

they realize how they improvise,
how the nails bite the wood

to such natural jazz, the house
rising tall in grace because of hard

music, lifting up its chimneyed head
and shoulders to the sky.

Sidekicks

It's tough to tell who's who.
One of us must star in this epic
with its cast of thousands, set against
this backdrop of the great unrest while
the other has the runny nose, the sputtering car,
the voice always squeaking toward falsetto.

Perhaps we're best off not knowing – I'll burn
the beans and flapjacks in the campfire skillet
while you go wrestle rustlers off a cliff,
tie my own laces together for laughs
while you grip evil with a single hand
by the scruff of its oily neck;

then it's your turn to wear the big face
and loud tie, make jokes through a mouthful
of doughnuts while I complete my memoir, perfect
my perfect sideburns with a razor in the mirror.

The Greatest Day in the World

No one said anything
with air quotes.

Worms rejoiced
in their silence.

Cows sang
the fields to sleep.

The air glittered
with beautiful insects.

Whales lifted themselves
like blessings from the sea

and La Pieta ceased
her weeping, rose stiffly

from her marble stool,
let her burden clatter

to the floor while
in Washington

Lincoln stood up
as well, loped off

toward the distant trees,
his giant stone hand

waving kindly and slow,
forgiving us all the idiocy.

IV

The Family Name

I'd wanted to give you my name
as a gift so you would be forever
known as a kind of me, only different,
better, if you want to know the truth,
but after all these married years
you still insist on being called
the daughter of your father,
who sits now at the window
in a fat ray of sun,
remembering the bright music
of your birth as dust planets
orbit the tiny universe,
the old clock folds the hour
inside itself yet again,
the slipcovers fade
and all the little brown bottles
line up in a careful row,
each labeled by the druggist
with the necessary warning
and the recommended dosage
underneath the family name.

The Sleeping Porch

There is the cat nestled lazy on the daybed,
the book left open spine up - dead bird
on the beach, the reach of afternoon sun
caught in the nets of window screen

skittering over the floorboards
towards the dark side of the world
and I just want to freeze this forever,
freeze the sun, the way you lie,

one elbow cocked, hand still cupped
around the shape of empty air
as the barometer slides down
its little glass ladder of numbers,

the sky hangs out its weary sheets, the wind
like the lonesome voice of everything
careening off the ceiling of a three-walled room
and even the furniture is turning into rain.

High Dark Windows

After our fight I stormed down
to the basement to crease my anger
by folding the laundry, fuming
among our mutual fabrics,
but there was your stained sweatshirt,
both arms entwined around the leg
of my brown cords and all that
interlocking underwear everywhere.

We are one creature, my love,
the dryer knows it and so does the bed
where we will lie again tonight
behind the high dark windows.

The wind will creak the clapboards softly,
jets flying overhead will cut their engines,
the owl, knowing who, will not ask why,
the clock will tick till the batteries die
and we will sleep the same exact sleep,
snore rough syncopated songs, wake up
to the same dawn with the same morning
mouth, bad hair, same lost smile between us.

Roadkill

We can't avoid the raccoon burst
like a melon, the squirrel that charmed us
in the park exploded into scraps of red fur
after it threw itself under somebody's tires,

someone who was driving a bit below
the speed limit with seat belt firmly locked,
hands on the wheel at ten and two o'clock,
the radio glossy with song,

the ashtray used only for toll basket change,
on their way to the corner store perhaps,
where they hoped to purchase a quart
of chocolate ice cream to celebrate

the end of another day in a fabulous life
wild with sky and bloody wonder.

Crank Calls

My heart has got me by the throat
and I want to see you so naked
not even skin will obstruct the view.

I drive all day to the corner store,
past lives rusted and greased.
When I step on the brake my life

is in my foot's hands, my eyes twin fires
in the chambered cave of my head.
Your morbific smile, your hypotonic jaw,

the way your bones connect to stone.
I spread your face across the sky,
hear voices in the dial tone.

Attic Calendars

Because I need to recall what it felt like
to live through Wednesday, March 9th, 1996,
the way it pressed against my shoulders,
its hours lodged in my shoe like small stones.

Because in some distant toothless future
I will need to know that Friday, May 28th, 1989
was when I had my mouth caressed
by the gentle fingers of a dental assistant
long folded now into memory's shadow of itself.

Because my instructions to the bereaved,
from whom I must eventually be torn like a page,
are to read aloud how I was proud to gather
the harvest of dry cleaning, was the one among
many who drove up smartly for the oil change
on time, made the lunch plans and kept them,
took pains to log in the latitude & longitude
of wherever I thought I heading.

Heartleaf Popple

Be my tree,
the last left standing
in the clearcut blotch.

I will kiss mystery
in your branches,
tines

sharp as starbeams
carving this night.
Let the idiocy of poems

guide us both into silence;
sculpture of cloudshape
is the drifted face

of the past,
its vast blindness
staining everything;

even as your eyes
touch these words
the heartleaf popple

plunges the wind, its shape
like the question mark
that ends every sentence.

Burning Leaves

I have come back home to be twelve again,
a graying kid too big for his bike,
bent like a tree in wet snow.

All the beds and mirrors have shrunk;
the dog who has been dead for decades
wags a withered tail.

My dead mother raises white-gloved hands
in surprise, pillbox hat cresting her coif
like a bright pink idea,

and next door they're burning
leaves in the late afternoon;
smoke filters broken sunlight,

a smell like the quiet taste of years
that brown to the ground to be gathered up
innocuously by someone in a dream about fire.

Persistence of Memory

Every morning I walk out
into my life again
stare hard at the edges
of everything
to frame its perfection
at being what it is
a perfect everything
in memory's dark rooms
if I should die and lie
on the other side of the lawn
dreaming sunflowers
bits of green glass
birds flying over water
the sound of the sky
the thousands of faces
I saw and never knew
to teach myself
how my heart is wider
than my life could ever be
how I'll have to be dead
probably forever
to remember all of it.

Everybody

Rises up each night like steam
            innocent and forgiven
                    for all the stupid choices

only to touch down again
            each morning.
                    And it is night right now

on half of the world
            half of everybody is rising
                    into the black sky

even as you read this
            half of everybody is
                    touching down again

ready or not to walk out
            into the glaring light
                    still yearning to lie

in the top rooms of houses
            cradled by rooftops
                    lifted by love of something

that has no name
            to swim like beauty
                    through the silent stars.

Toy Firing Squad

Back on your knees
on the tundra of linoleum,
chest out, hands twined behind,
about to die
for the fourth time today;

imaginary cigarette refused again,
blindfold of knotted socks ignored,
the twelve plastic soldiers burning up
to kill you,
faces clenched in clotted bloodrage,
rifles, flame throwers, even a hand grenade
aimed precisely at the bullseye
crudely painted on your heart

and you glance up as I walk in,
smile sadly about bullets
fathers must bite,
then jolt and writhe gutshot
on the floor once more
to your kid's ancient squeals
of delight.

Aftermath

There is the man who repairs the shoes
he could never afford and the man who
prepares the food he is unprepared to eat.

And there is the red kneed woman
who washes the floors of the rooms
she is not allowed to enter in daylight.

There is the one who hangs from a harness
to scrape the windows of the penthouse suite
and overhear the glib jokes of millionaires.

And there is the one who stirs the drinks,
knows the fumbling of meaningless hands,
ripe breath of longing.

Someone must serve as the king's
first taster and someone account
for the accountant's suicide.

And there is the woman who must scrub
the toilet she is not permitted to sit upon
but does anyway, and feels for a moment

the way the perfect feel always,
and in aftermath perhaps a quiet dignity
that lasts for a good twenty minutes.

To the Unkilled

Who accompany the caskets home,
each one with identical flag disguise,
each one exactly the same amount dead.

Who pull up to houses in government sedans,
check their nails, the razored creases of their trousers,
check their eyes in the reflection of their shoes.

Who march up the walk to the front steps to bear
the brunt of the first reaction, the ashen implosion,
the screams that crackle the neighborhood sky.

Who stand erect at the lip of each grave,
as graves have lips and are a mouth,
snap the flag from the coffin lid,

fold it precisely, a problem of geometry,
then offer the small triangle of stars
as if it was a broken piece of night.

Tao of the Yo

Every time I try to yo yo
I only manage to yo.

The plastic disk hangs at the end
of the string like a dead planet
too far away from any sun to care.

Eventually it crawls halfway back up,
a kind of victory over itself,
then slumps and dangles limp again.

I've learned to push water out of my way,
to blow pink clouds of gum, learned
the windy rush of handlebars
with only two wheels
and at some point overdosed
on the medicine that cures nothing,
the love that makes everyone dance
at the end of a bouncing thread.

But what I've never understood and clearly still don't
is how a simple flick of the proper wrist
can make what you set free return to your hand,
rock the baby in the cradle, glow in the dark
and walk the whole damn dog around the world.

Midweek Poem

I crawled outside my body
through my mouth and fingers,
out both ears,
waited in air
while I did a crossword,
filed my nails, told a small lie,
ate part of a salad,
then crawled back in
and slept through the night,
silent as a chair in a darkened room,
completely forgetting this dream of itself
before I awoke the next morning.

My Martini

Shaken to its bones,
each molecule of vodka
a memory,
Zhivago's yellow fields
pushed against unsmiling sky.

There is ice lodged in this story,
a thousand unwritten winters
frozen past all suffering, the snow falling
through the years muffling the widow's tears,
piled bodies, the smoking rubble of palaces.

And, of course, an amnesia of vermouth,
with one olive more than happy to flood my skull
with fire, one to numb the world into a silly toy
and one impaled on a plastic prong
in the shape of a tiny sword.

Abbey Road

We once crossed this street in single file,
pastor, undertaker, gravedigger, corpse,
scuffling bare feet across the crosswalk,
a Volkswagen humped at the curb with
28 IF on its plate; we once arrived too late
to be part of the funeral of music never
imagined, where dirt was tossed into hope's
open casket, candlelight vigils went dark
in the park, shots got shot into ghosts
we wished we could see, really see,
thin as wire, sleek as neon, wearing
shades at night, hung dark with silence
and stained black with blood, wild
like wind sweeping what's coming at us
toward where we no longer belong:
inside some lost song remembered then
forgotten then remembered then gone.

Be Thanking

Sometimes I am being like all thanking and thanking
like when I am alone in a field or looking at one
and sometimes I am looking at the fields of sea
and like thanking and thanking you for what is under
everything but darkness.

And when the goatskin is being empty
and I am inside my stomach swimming
in the red wine I am also being
like all thanking and thanking you
who hides behind the blue sky,
behind my aching
and then I am to lick my paw
and be thanking and thanking
because nothing tastes as good
or as bad.

Tom Chandler is poet laureate of Rhode Island emeritus. He has been named Phi Beta Kappa Poet at Brown University and has been a featured poet at the Robert Frost homestead. His poems have been read by Garrison Keillor on National Public Radio. *Toy Firing Squad* is his fifth book.

CPSIA information can be obtained at www.ICGtesting.com
Printed in the USA
BVOW03s0210180614

356702BV00001B/6/P